# so you want to write Poetry

## Brian Moses

Schools Library and Information Services

Other title in the series:
So You Want To Write Fiction

Text © Brian Moses 2003
Editor: Gill Munton
Designer: Sarah Borny

Published in Great Britain in 2003 by Hodder Wayland,
an imprint of Hodder Children's Books
This paperback edition published in 2004

The website address (URLs) included in this book were valid at
the time of going to press. However, because of the nature of the Internet,
it is possible that some addresses have changed, or sites may have
changed or closed down since publication. While the author and Publisher
regret any inconvenience this may cause readers, no responsibility for any
such changes can be accepted by either the author or the Publisher.

A Catalogue record for this book is available from the British Library.

ISBN:   07502 36469(hb)
        07502 38585(pb)

Printed in Hong Kong

Hodder Children's Books
A division of Hodder Headline Limited
338 Euston Road, London NW1 3BH

# Contents

# Introduction

## So you want to write poetry?

First of all, let's try this simple test.

- ◎ **Do you like stringing words together to find out what they look like and what they sound like?**

- ◎ **Do you have rhythms dancing in your head as you drift through the day?**

- ◎ **Do people tell you that you're a dreamer and that you should keep your feet on the ground?**

- ◎ **Do you find yourself bursting with creative ideas when you're in the bath, or standing in a bus queue?**

- ◎ **Does your brain complain as you write through the night?**

- ◎ **Do you rhyme all the time while your feet tap a beat?**

If you answered "yes" to all or most of these questions, you're probably hooked on words and poetry.

## Do you enjoy reading poetry?

Just as reading fiction will help you with your story writing, reading poetry is important if you want to develop as a poet. Don't stick to one sort of poetry; don't just read Ted Hughes, or Michael Rosen, or traditional poetry, or "modern stuff".

Read everything; read as widely as you can. Make up anthologies of favourite poems that you discover in your reading. Try to work out why you like these particular poems, how they make you feel, and what kind of style the poet has written in.

## Why do people write poetry?

Now ask yourself why you want to write poetry.

Read what some poets say about their reasons:

I have a theory that everyone in the world likes to make something. For some people it's a dress, or a table, a model, or a picture. I like to take piles of words and make a poem.

*Judith Nicholls*

I write poems in order to entertain and to make people think.

*John Foster*

I like being able to say a lot in just a few words, and I love building many layers of meaning into one piece of writing.

*Valerie Bloom*

If I didn't, I think I'd explode.

*Charles Causley*

It is the excitement of starting with a blank page and seeing a poem grow and develop on that page, a poem that no one else on Planet Earth has written before.

*Wes Magee*

# Getting ideas

## Keeping an ideas notebook

An ideas notebook is a treasure chest of ideas that you can dip into when you are thinking about writing a poem.

A poet needs to be ready to write down any scrap of inspiration the moment it occurs. Some poets carry notebooks around with them. Others scribble away on whatever they find in their pockets – old envelopes, till receipts, bus tickets – and transfer their ideas to a notebook later. I'm always finding odd bits of paper on which I've scribbled ideas which I then transfer to an A4 notebook. It's up to you, but if you want to write poetry in a serious way, an ideas notebook is essential.

Your notebook will probably contain all or some of the following:

- Half-completed poems (a few lines that you thought sounded good but didn't know what do with at the time)
- Quotes from other people's poems or stories that you've copied down as inspiration
- Jokes
- Jingles
- Adverts
- Unusual shop signs and street names
- Cuttings from newspapers or magazines
- Snippets of overheard conversations (Once, when I passed a little boy and his mother in the street, I overheard the boy say, "Mummy, did pirates wear nail varnish?" I wrote that down and later on I used it as the first line in a poem.)

Think about your day, and make notes about anything interesting that you have heard or seen. (Don't expect to be able to use all these ideas in poems.) Don't worry about keeping your notes neat and tidy. This is *your* notebook. There's nobody standing behind you with a red pen. You may need to write quickly when the ideas are flowing; as long as you can read what you have written, that's all that matters.

If you keep an ideas notebook, you will never be sitting there wondering what to write about. You can flick through your notebook, and something will grab your attention. Before you know it, you'll be taking a fresh look at what you wrote and feeling inspired to take it further. The few lines that you started with may well turn into a complete poem.

## Using a dictaphone

Later on, if you get really serious about your writing, you may like to buy a dictaphone for recording your ideas. They are not very expensive, and are useful if your ideas come more quickly than you can write them down. I've used a dictaphone for many years, and I certainly wouldn't want to be without one.

# Getting ideas

## When an idea comes knocking

An idea is a bit like a knock on the door. Ignore the knocking, and whoever it is will go away. Ignore the idea, and it will go away, too. Ideas don't always come along at convenient times. You may be walking down the street, or running to school, or lying in the bath, or dreaming during Maths. Whatever you're doing, you will need to jot something down on paper as soon as you can. I have a big pile of old envelopes in my kitchen, and I'm always scribbling on the backs of those.

Don't ignore your dreams, either. Crazy things happen in dreams, and if you try to remember yours, there may be inspiration for your poetry in them. There's a notebook on my bedside table, just in case I need to write down some ideas as soon as I wake up!

## Ideas are all around us

The places you visit can give you ideas for poems. I find holidays particularly fruitful. A poem of mine called "The Lost Angels" was inspired by three turtles in an aquarium in France, and notes for a poem called "Sheep on Snowdon" were made as I travelled up Snowdon on the mountain railway. I have also written about the seagulls in St. Ives, the castle on Guernsey and a cable-car in the Alps. All new experiences are valuable to the writer.

Another idea for a poem came when I was visiting New York with the writer Pie Corbett. We were walking down Madison Avenue when we spotted a sign on a lamppost saying, "Lost cat - $500 reward". We both knew that we wanted to write about the lost cat in New York, and we ended up writing a poem together.

# Are you an observer?

Train yourself to be an observer – to be an ideas detective. Look for possibilities everywhere and in everything. Train yourself to look closely at something and to see what it reminds you of. Brainstorm ideas and write them down. Brainstorming is probably one of the things that you do at school when your teacher asks you to write a poem, as it is an excellent way to get started.

For example, collect words to describe thistles:

- "sharp"
- "prickly"
- "spiteful" (the kind of leaf that gets its own back on anyone who picks it!)

Now think of some creatures that thistles remind you of:

- hedgehogs
- echidnas
- porcupines
- dragons

Perhaps the poet Stanley Cook began in a similar way when he wrote this poem about thistles:

### Thistles

*Thistles are dragons growing wild*
*In the wind on the hillside,*
*Fierce green dragons*
*With prickling stalks for legs*
*And leaves for wings with a prickly edge.*
*With a flower like purple fire*
*They burn in fields or beside the road,*
*Puffing out thistledown seeds*
*That blow away like smoke.*

**Stanley Cook**

9

# Getting ideas

## Finding something fresh to say

What shall I write about? If you have your ideas notebook up and running, you'll probably have realised by now that you don't need to ask yourself that question very often.

Once you have a subject, you will need to consider how you can make that subject interesting. It is easy – too easy – to take a subject such as winter, and then to trot out a series of ideas that everyone has heard before.

There are so many poems that give us a Christmas card image of winter, whereas real winter is often very different from this. It may be cold winds and endless rainy days, damp mornings, dark afternoons, steamy windows and mud in school. Ask yourself whether you are being honest in your writing, and then try to find something fresh to say. A poem about winter could begin in this way:

*At the end of September, Wayne caught the cold that lasted through till May.*
*He coughed and spluttered, choked and wheezed, sneezed noisily all day.*
*When Wayne blew his nose I'd only heard something similar once before,*
*as the QE2 left Southampton and its hooter gave a roar.*

If you can, then, try to find a less obvious route to a poem. If you are writing about fireworks you could find a fresh angle – describing fireworks from an animal's point of view, or writing about the debris of used fireworks on the morning after Bonfire Night. It is the different approach that will get you noticed as a writer.

Here are two more examples:

> *The dinosaurs are not all dead,*
> *I saw one raise its iron head …*
>
> From *"Steam Shovel"*
> by Charles Malam

> *And there's a ruined holy city*
> *In a herd of lying down, cud-chewing cows …*
>
> From *"What is the Truth?"*
> by Ted Hughes

## Sifting the ideas

You may find that with some poems it is almost as if a button has been pushed in your brain, releasing a flow of words and ideas that is very hard to turn off. You find yourself frantically trying to keep pace with fresh ideas as they tumble on to the page. Your next task is to rearrange the ideas, discarding those which don't really work. Remember that what you take out of a poem is often just as important to the poem's structure as the ideas that you leave in. In the words of the famous poet Samuel Taylor Coleridge, "Poetry is the best words in the best order".

Make a list of five places that you have visited recently, perhaps on a day trip or a holiday. Think of something special about each place – something surprising or weird, something sad, or something that made you laugh. Pick your best idea, and brainstorm further ideas. String them together to make a poem.

# Structuring a poem

## Using a model

It is sometimes a good idea to model a poem on one which has been written by another writer. This will help you to focus on the structure. Many writers begin by modelling their own work on that of others until they eventually develop their own style.

Look for a poem which follows a clear pattern on which you can "hang" your own ideas. You could try this with a poem called "Dragons' Wood". This poem doesn't rhyme but it does have a strong rhythm. As you read the poem, you will notice that the first and last verses begin with the words "We didn't see …" and the verses in between begin with the words "We saw …" This repetition helps to give the poem its rhythm.

### Dragons' Wood

We didn't see dragons
in Dragons' Wood
but we saw
where the dragons had been.

We saw tracks in soft mud
that could only have been left
by some sharp-clawed creature.

We saw scorched earth
where fiery dragon breath
had whitened everything to ash.

We saw trees burnt to charcoal.
We saw dragon dung
rolled into boulders.

And draped from a branch
we saw sloughed off skin,
scaly, still warm …

We didn't see dragons
in Dragons' Wood,
but this was the closest
we'd ever been

to believing.

Brian Moses

---

**Write more poems in this way. You could write about Witches' Wood, Devils' Dyke, Mermaids' Lagoon, Trolls' Tor, Giants' Crag …**

**Your poem could begin in this way:**

We didn't see giants
on Giants' Crag
but we saw
where the giants had been.

We saw ….

## Building the poem up

When you have written a poem, ask yourself whether it looks like a poem on the page. A poem isn't just prose that has been cut up to make it look like a poem. A poem is a poem right from the start. It is important to think carefully about where the line breaks should be. Line breaks help a reader to understand how the poet wants the poem to be read because they indicate where to pause and take a breath. They can also promote the rhythm of the poem.

In the example on the right, Holly Delafield has patterned her poem by writing her first idea in the first line and then developing it in the second. She has followed this pattern all the way through the poem.

### Spirit of the Moon

*The ghostly spirit of the moon*

*Wears an icy cloak of shimmering and sparkly star dust.*

*Her long silver hair cascades down past her feet*

*Like a shining waterfall of glass.*

*Her skin is a pale shade of midnight blue*

*And her eyes are stony ebony upon her pale face.*

*Her proud lips are like the early morning frost*

*As cold and hard as white marble.*

*Thin, icy fingers and jagged nails clasp*

*A crystal stone, the colour of the night sky.*

*She glides along the ground like a running stream,*

*Her thin, blue feet making no sound.*

*When she speaks it is like a breath of the wind,*

*Husky, like a spirit of the dead.*

**Holly Delafield**
*Much Marcle*
*Primary School*

# What about rhyme?

**A poem doesn't have to rhyme, but an effective rhyming poem can chime and ring as the words work together in surprising ways. It can give a musical quality to a poem, which makes it easy to read and remember. Advertisers know how effective rhyme can be when they compose their slogans, and so do song writers when they are looking for a chorus that will stay in people's minds when the song is over.**

## Ways of rhyming

There are various ways of using rhyme in poetry. Here are some examples.

If you use rhyming couplets, the first line rhymes with the second, the third with the fourth, and so on.

*I didn't like it, not one bit,*
*webs hung down from the ceiling and hit*
*the side of your face as you travelled past*
*ever so slowly – oh, can't we go fast? -*

*on the g-g-g-g-g-g-g-ghost train.*

Another way is to make the second and fourth lines (or the first and third lines) rhyme.

*Last year's new beginning*
*didn't last for very long.*
*I kept my part of the bargain, Mum,*
*but where did you go wrong?*

In this five-line verse, the second line rhymes with the fifth and the third with the fourth.

*I'm thinking of Christmas morning*
*and all the presents I'll find,*
*but what if I've missed*
*something good off my list?*
*- it keeps going round in my mind.*

## Finding the right rhyme

As you write, keep asking yourself whether you have found the right rhyme. A weak rhyme can spoil a poem, and it is worth searching for the best possible one. You may find that you need to change the whole line before you can find a rhyme that works.

If you are really stuck, try using a rhyming dictionary. For example, you need a rhyme for "feet" but the ones that you've thought of – "eat", "heat", "meet", "sleet", "street" – don't fit the poem. Look up the word "feet" (or the sound "eet", depending on the dictionary). You will find a list of rhymes from "Crete", "cheat" and "wheat" to "incomplete", "deadbeat" and "lorikeet".

(A lorikeet, by the way, is a small parrot!)

Collect examples of different kinds of rhyming poetry, and make up an anthology. Look for traditional poems as well as modern material. Identify the rhyme scheme used by each poet. Can you find any really unusual rhyme schemes?

# Rapping

"**R**apping" means "speaking rhythmically over a beat". It's a fun way of writing a performance poem. You have probably heard raps in many places – on the radio, on television, in record shops and clothes shops, in street performances.

Raps can be written about all kinds of topic. This one tells how the Roman soldiers hated life on Hadrian's Wall.

The soldiers on the Roman wall
really had no fun at all.
All they ever did was moan,
they knew they'd rather be at home.

*Chorus:*
Hey, ho, here we go,
another day of rain and snow.

If you want to write a rap, you need to tap out a rhythm first. When you're happy with it, try using an instrument such as a tambourine, a drum, claves or shakers. Alternatively, try rapping to the programmed rap track on a keyboard. Remember that if you use music, it should only be a background for the words. It is the words of your rap that are important, and you need to say them loudly enough to be heard.

This rap protests about parents!

Our parents tell us off a lot,
What makes them think that they're so hot?
Every night they lose the plot,
Perhaps their brains have started to rot.

Our parents make us eat our greens,
Carrots, tomatoes and runner beans.
I don't believe I've got their genes,
They even haunt us in our dreams.

*Chorus:*
Parents, parents
Always moan,
Make us fret,
Make us groan.

**Class 6**

*Groombridge St. Thomas C.E. School*

Raps rely on rhymes and very strong rhythms. You can get away with near-rhymes; in the second example on page 16, "dreams" is not an exact rhyme for "genes", but it is close enough. If you say it quickly, no one will notice!

## Try writing a rap about yourself ...

*My name is Paul and I'm five feet tall,*
*I'm fast as lightning, tough as a wall*

## ... or about your friends ...

*Martha, Linette, Kate and Davina*
*Make more noise than a vacuum cleaner*
*Sarah, Karen, Celine and Faye*
*Laze in bed for much of the day*

*Word is out on the street tonight,*
*Billy's coming back.*

*There's a sound outside of running feet,*
*somebody somewhere's switched on the heat,*
*policemen are beating a swift retreat,*
*now Billy's coming back ...*

# Useful techniques

## Similes

A simile is a comparison using the word "as" or "like". Similes are used to make interesting images.

Poets often use similes, but they should be original. Many of the similes you will hear in everyday speech have been used again and again, so there is no element of surprise:

*"When he saw the ghost he turned as white as a sheet."*

*"I looked into the cupboard but it was as black as ink."*

*"He's been no trouble – in fact, he's been as good as gold."*

A good simile in a poem should be a fresh simile:

*"as slow as ... a farmer pushing his tractor up a steep hill"*

*"as noisy as ... a volcano erupting into a microphone"*

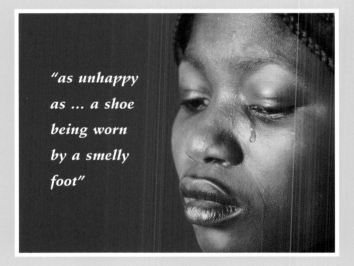

*"as unhappy as ... a shoe being worn by a smelly foot"*

## Metaphors

A metaphor is a direct comparison that doesn't rely on "as" or "like". In *Gulliver's Travels*, Jonathan Swift describes Gulliver as a "man mountain". A rolled up mattress could be "a huge Swiss roll". Metaphors about people can give us insights into their personalities. Perhaps your teacher can be an "angry wasp" on occasions!

Sometimes, a metaphor is extended throughout a complete poem. I once wrote a poem about a stern teacher I remembered from my childhood. I compared the look that she gave the children to the cold north face of a mountain, and then continued by using lots of words and phrases associated with mountains. Here is the beginning of the poem.

*This is the famous north face of our teacher*

*That's never been known to crack a smile.*

*This is the famous north face of our teacher,*

*Few have scaled the heights to please her.*

*Some of us have tried and failed,*

*Some of us knew we hadn't a hope,*

*Some of us were brushed aside,*

*Or slid back down the slippery slope.*

*The moon was a ghostly galleon*

*tossed upon cloudy seas*

**From *"The Highwayman"*
by Alfred Noyes**

## Personification

This is when a writer takes something that isn't human and then gives it human characteristics. A tree might be described as having "branches that finger the moon"; road diggers could "gulp up great gobfuls of mud"; the central heating system could be "coughing and spluttering".

Ellie Pratt makes excellent use of personification in the first two lines of her poem about an alleyway.

*The alleyway glowered like a moon without its shine.*
*The wall groaned with graffiti piled on top ...*

**Ellie Pratt**
*Kent College Junior School*

## Alliteration

Alliteration is the grouping of words which have the same first letter. It can be very effective in poetry, and is fun to do.

### The Playground Snake

*When the playground snake*
*slithered into school,*
*It scared all the teachers in the staff room,*
*It snaked through to the kitchen*
*and slurped the soup,*
*It stole the biscuits, soundlessly and secretly,*
*It spat as it slid slowly into Class 6,*
*It started to strangle the stressed secretary*
*Till finally it sneaked into the stock room*
*and snoozed on the shelves.*

Class 6

*Groombridge St. Thomas C.E. School*

Alternatively, you might give your poem an alliterative title such as "Sheep on Sheppey", "My Magnificent Maggot" or "Tests for Teachers".

*Them that asks no questions isn't told a lie –*

*Watch the wall, my darling,*

*while the Gentlemen go by.*

From *"A Smuggler's Song"*
by Rudyard Kipling

**Try to write four sentences about a tree using these four poetic techniques.**

*Simile*

**The tree is as tall as …**

or

**Its trunk is as thick as …**

*Metaphor*

**The tree is …**

*Personification*

**The leaves …**

*Alliteration*

**The branches …**

# Different poetic forms

**S**ome poems have very tight structures. Here are two examples.

## Haikus

*A neat acrobat*

*we applaud her skilful leap*

*to the highest branch*

**H**aiku is a traditional form of Japanese poetry. A haiku must have three lines containing seventeen syllables in total (five syllables in the first line, seven in the second, and five in the third).

Haikus are sometimes called "one-breath poems", as they are short enough to be spoken between one breath and the next. Haikus are really "word snapshots", giving the reader a picture in words of what is happening at a particular moment.

One way of working on a haiku is to look at a view and note down a number of things that can be seen. Then strike out words and phrases that don't add much to the picture until you are left with about ten words that best describe the scene. See if you can fit these words into the structure of a haiku.

## Acrostics

In an acrostic, the first letters of the lines spell out the subject of the poem. A well written acrostic should not be simply a random selection of lines; each line should have some connection with the one that went before. You could challenge yourself by trying to write a rhyming acrostic. In this example, the first, second and fifth lines rhyme, as do the third and fourth.

### April

**A**pril is a troublesome mix of sudden
   showers and sun,
**P**laying with our hopes for fine weather,
   now that winter's done.
**R**uining picnics, dampening dreams,
**I**t's a month that isn't quite what it seems
**L**eading us to warmer days
   and hinting at summer fun.

**Try writing a haiku or an acrostic.**

# Redrafting

## Practical tips

**1** Think back to Coleridge's definition of poetry: "Poetry is the best words in the best order." In a poem, every word should be pulling its weight; it should be there because it helps the poem. Kick out any words that hinder the poem's flow, words that just don't sound right when you read them.

**2** Identify any weak words and phrases and replace them with more interesting ones. Don't settle for ordinary words like "walking" or "talking" when an alternative could add colour or surprise to what you have written. Look at this example:

*"The ghost went down*

*the staircase."*

Replace "went", which is a dull word, with "floated", "drifted", "flowed" or "slunk" – something that defines more accurately the movement of the ghost on the stairs.

There is always a better word for "nice" or "great big", and it is the poet's task to find it.

**3** See if there are any words that have been used too many times. Unless you have deliberately repeated words or phrases to assist the rhythm of a poem, you will need to change words that reappear. It is easy to repeat adjectives or adverbs without realising.

**4** Don't be content with clichés – stale or tired ideas. We all use clichés in everyday conversation, but there should be no place for them in your poems. If you've heard an idea before, your readers will have heard it, too. Get rid of it, and think of a fresh one.

**5** Don't use two words for the same idea. In the phrase "the tired, weary horse", "tired" and "weary" mean the same thing, so the poem will benefit by losing one of them.

## Feedback

When you have written a poem, you are probably too close to it, too protective of it, to be able to look at it critically. You need someone else who can see it with fresh eyes and tell you what does and what doesn't work.

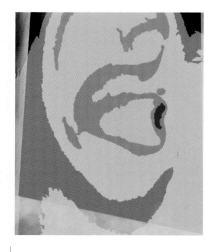

Show your poem to a family member or a friend. Perhaps you have a friend who also enjoys writing. It would be a great help if you could support each other by commenting on each other's work.

I usually read new poems to my wife, Anne. She will say what she likes about a poem, but she will be honest and tell me if there is something she doesn't like. She's usually right, although I may be reluctant to take her advice if I happen to like that particular section of the poem.

# Your audience

## Reading your work aloud

At first, you may feel like keeping your poems hidden away in notebooks and not showing them to anyone. One day, however, you will probably want to take that first step and test them on an audience, perhaps family members or friends.

If you have read in school assemblies or events for parents, you will know a little about how nervous reading to an audience can make you feel. When you read your own work, you may feel even more vulnerable as you will be worried about how your audience will react to your poems. Try to look confident, even if you're not, and try to sound confident as you read. The more you practise your poems, the more familiar you will be with them and the more confident you will appear.

Be proud of what you have written. Never start by saying, "I don't think this is very good, but I'll read it anyway." Let your audience be the judge; it is their opinions that you are after.

Read your poem clearly and loudly. Remember Grandma, who may be a little hard of hearing, at the back of the room. She will want to hear you, too. If there are lines in your poem designed to make your audience laugh, don't be surprised if they do just that. Don't rush on – pause, and enjoy the laughter.

## Asking for a response

If you have asked for a critical response, listen carefully to what is said. If someone

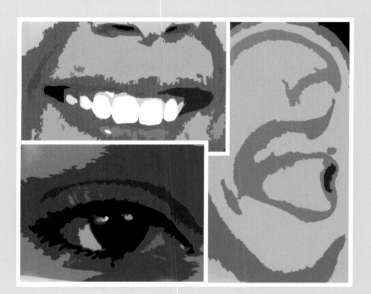

makes a criticism, don't feel that your poem isn't any good. Response to poetry is very subjective. This means that what one person dislikes, someone else may enjoy. I have had huge amounts of criticism of my poetry in the past, and I still get reviews in which critics are less than complimentary. Consider what is said, but feel free to reject it. If you really want to write, you will keep on writing whatever anyone says.

## Tape recording your poems

A good way of improving your ability to read aloud effectively is to tape record your poems. When you play a poem back, you should be able to hear whether some parts are being read too quickly so that their impact is lost. You can judge where you need to put more expression into your voice, and where you need to pause for effect.

You could also practise saying something about each poem – perhaps describing how you came to write it. Many poets are good raconteurs; they can tell entertaining stories to introduce their poems. Setting a poem in its context can help your audience to appreciate it fully.

# Getting noticed

**O**ne question I'm often asked by children and their parents is, **"How can I get my poems published?"**

## Books, magazines and comics

Sending your poems to a book publisher would not really be the best option. It is unlikely (but not totally impossible) that an editor would consider publishing a collection of poetry by one child. He or she will probably respond with an encouraging letter, but please don't hope for much more.

Look out for magazines and comics that print the occasional poem. For example, a magazine about animals might use poems about the animals that are featured. Children's newspapers come and go, but these are publications that may well consider using some poetry. There are also a few magazines devoted to children's writing. (For their addresses, see page 32.) All of these will consider your writing.

## Websites

It is well worth looking for children's poetry websites on the Internet (see page 32). Some of them, such as the Poetry Zone, accept poetry written by children, and it can be exciting to see your poems published

on the Internet. On many of the websites you can read interviews with children's poets as well as their poetry. Many poets have their own sites, and these are worth a visit.

## Opportunities in school

If your school has a magazine, it may have a poetry section. If not, suggest starting one, and say that you would be happy to be the poetry editor. If your school doesn't have a magazine, you could offer to start one up.

Consider producing a poetry booklet. This could simply be a few photocopied pages, or, if you have access to desktop publishing facilities, you could produce something a little more professional. This could be sold to cover your costs, or given away to family members and friends. Before you print your booklet, check your poems carefully for spelling errors and misplaced words.

## Competitions

Look out for poetry competitions in magazines and newspapers and on the Internet. It is worth entering your work, as the publications often print booklets in association with the competitions. Even if your poems don't win a prize, they may be featured. Keep a record of your successes, to impress publishers when you feel that you are ready to start sending them your work.

Finally, don't be tempted to pay to see your work in print. A publication may not pay you for your poem – although you should receive a free copy of any book or magazine in which it appears – but your work will be valued on its own merit and not because you have paid someone to use it.

Remember, if you want to be a writer … write!

### Good luck!

# Glossary

**acrostic** — a short poem in which the first letters of the lines form a word when read vertically

**alliteration** — the grouping of words which begin with the same letter

**cliché** — a tired, stale image

**haiku** — a poem in a traditional Japanese style which has 17 syllables (five in the first line, seven in the second and five in the third)

**metaphor** — a direct comparison which doesn't rely on "as" or "like"

**personification** — a description which refers to something non-human in human terms

**rap** — a punchy, rhyming poem which is spoken fast

**rhyme** — the repetition of stressed vowels and their following consonants

**rhythm** — a regular beat in music or poetry

**simile** — a comparison between two things which uses "as" or "like"

# Index

# Resources

## Your writer's library

This should include a good dictionary, a thesaurus and a rhyming dictionary. A practical book on grammar and an encyclopedia would be useful, too.

Read the companion book to this, *So You Want To Write Fiction* by Tony Bradman (Hodder Wayland).

*Favourite Poets* by Brian Moses (Hodder Wayland) features interviews with a number of children's poets including Roger McGough, Benjamin Zephaniah and Charles Causley.

Make a collection of poetry in a variety of styles. Poets you could consider including are: Ted Hughes, Charles Causley, Roger McGough, Gareth Owen, Kit Wright, Valerie Bloom, John Agard, Grace Nichols, Judith Nicholls, Wes Magee, Peter Dixon, Tony Mitton and Michael Rosen. Look out for anthologies edited by John Foster, Anne Harvey, Fiona Waters, Paul Cookson – and, of course, me! (I'm Brian Moses, by the way, in case you'd forgotten!)

## Useful addresses

### Magazines

**Young Writer**
Glebe House
Weobley
Herefordshire HR4 8SD

Tel: 01544 318901
Website: **www.mystworld.com/youngwriter**

This is a specialist magazine for young writers aged 6-16, featuring interviews with top children's writers and giving children opportunities to see their own prose and poetry in print. Three issues are published each year.

**Wordsmith** and **Scribbler**
c/o Young Writers
Remus House
Coltsfoot Drive
Woodston
Peterborough PE2 9JX

Tel: 01733 890066
e-mail: **youngwriters@forwardpress.co.uk**

Both magazines feature advice for young writers, interviews and opportunities for work to be published. *Wordsmith* is for children aged 12 and above, and *Scribbler* is for a younger readership. Both are published four times a year.

### Websites

**The Poetry Zone**
**www.poetryzone.ndirect.co.uk**

This is run by the children's poet Roger Stevens, and features many children's poets plus the opportunity to see your poems published on the Internet.

You may also want to look at some publishers' websites:
**www.hodderheadline.co.uk**
**www.puffin.co.uk**
**www.panmacmillan.com**

## Acknowledgements

The author and publisher would like to thank the following for permission to reproduce copyright material:

**Extracts**

**P7** Macmillan Children's Books for "The Sea Creature" from *Barking Back at Dogs* by Brian Moses
**P9** Stanley Cook for "Thistles" from *The Squirrel in Town and Other Nature Poems* by Stanley Cook
**P11** Harcourt Publishers for the extract from "Steam Shovel" by Charles Malam
**P11** Faber & Faber Ltd for the extract from "What is the Truth?" by Ted Hughes
**P12** Macmillan Children's Books for "Dragons' Wood" from *Barking Back at Dogs* by Brian Moses
**P13** Holly Delafield for "Spirit of the Moon"
**P16, p20** Groombridge St Thomas CE School for "Our Parents" and "The Playground Snake"
**P19** The Society of Authors as the Literary Representative of Alfred Noyes for the extract from "The Highwayman" by Alfred Noyes
**P20** Ellie Pratt for the extract from "The Alleyway"
**P21** AP Watt Ltd on behalf of The National Trust for Places of Historical Interest or Natural Beauty for the extract from "A Smuggler's Song" by Rudyard Kipling

All unattributed poems and extracts by Brian Moses

**Photographs and illustrations**

**P9** Oxford Scientific Library
**P10, p15, p17, p19, p21, p25, p27, p28** Martyn Chillmaid
**P18, p20, p22, p23, p26** Corbis

While every effort has been made to obtain permission, there may still be cases in which we have failed to trace a copyright holder. The publisher will be happy to correct any omission in future reprintings.